The North Carolina Poems

The North Carolina Poems

A. R. Ammons

A NEW EDITION

*Edited with an Afterword
by Alex Albright*

BROADSTONE BOOKS

Most of these poems have appeared previously in books
by A.R. Ammons published by W·W·Norton & Company.
See Acknowledgments (pages ix–x) for details.

LC: 2010933286

ISBN: 978-0-9802117-2-6

COVER PHOTOGRAPH COURTESY OF VIDA AMMONS COX

Copyright © 2010 by John Ammons

See page ix (Acknowledgments) for a listing
of all rights and permissions

BROADSTONE BOOKS
AN IMPRINT OF BROADSTONE MEDIA LLC
418 ANN STREET
FRANKFORT, KY 40601-1929
BroadstoneBooks.com

CONTENTS

I WENT BACK   3
FIRST CAROLINA SAID-SONG   4
CHISELED CLOUDS   6
I BROKE A SHEAF OF LIGHT   7
MY FATHER USED TO TELL OF AN   8
INTERVAL   11
FATHER   13
HELP   14
WHEN I WAS YOUNG UNDER THE APPLE   15
MOTIONING   19
MEMORIES, TAPESTRIES   21
MAKING FIELDS   27
MY FATHER USED TO BRING BANANA   29
MY FATHER, I HOLLOW FOR YOU   31
FOR MY BELOVED SON   32
EASTER MORNING   33
SURPRISING ELEMENTS   37
NELLY MYERS   39
ROSALIE   44
HARDWEED PATH GOING   45
MULE SONG   48
WE LOST OUR MULE KATE   49
SILVER   52
UNCLE JOHN WAS   54
I'M THE TYPE   56

BROAD BRUSH   59

COON SONG   61

MEDICINE FOR TIGHT SPOTS   64

BODY MARKS   66

THE CONSTANT   68

DEFINITIONS   70

TRANSFER   71

THE NEXT DAY   72

THE QUINCE BUSH   73

LOFTY CALLING   75

SIGHT SEED   76

TROUBLE MAKING TROUBLE   77

GOT TO LEAVE   78

CHRISTMAS EVE   82

TODAY IS DIM AGAIN   85

MOTION FOR MOTION   92

RECORDING   95

COMMISSARY   96

SECOND CAROLINA SAID-SONG   97

THE YUCCA MOTH   99

SIGNIFICANCES   100

MEDIATION   101

FOR EMILY WILSON FROM A NEWCOMER   102

GRAVELLY RUN   103

YADKIN PICNIC   105

CASCADILLA FALLS   106

DISHES AND DASHES   108

KEEPING TRACK   110

BETWEEN EACH SONG   111

WHAT ARE WE TO THINK?   113

LIFE IN THE BOONDOCKS   120

ALLIGATOR HOLES DOWN ALONG ABOUT OLD DOCK   121

WHEN I WAS YOUNG THE SILK   122

CHINABERRY   123

AFTERWORD   127

ACKNOWLEDGMENTS

'I Went Back' reprinted from *Worldly Hopes* by A.R. Ammons ©1982 by A.R. Ammons, by permission of W·W·Norton & Company, Inc.

'Memories, Tapestries,' 'We lost our mule Kate,' 'Got to leave' and 'Today is dim again' reprinted from *Tape for the Turn of the Year* by A.R. Ammons © 1965 by A.R. Ammons, by permission of W·W·Norton & Company, Inc.

'Motioning' reprinted from *Lake Effect Country* by A.R. Ammons © 1983 by A.R. Ammons, by permission of W·W·Norton & Company, Inc.

'Father,' 'Medicine for Tight Spots,' 'The Quince Bush,' 'Transfer' reprinted from *Briefings* by A.R. Ammons © 1971 by A.R. Ammons, by permission of W·W·Norton & Company, Inc.

'Recording' and 'Mediation' reprinted from *The Really Short Poems* by A.R. Ammons © 1990 by A.R. Ammons, by permission of W·W·Norton & Company, Inc.

'What are we to think' reprinted from *Garbage* by A.R. Ammons © 1993 by A.R. Ammons, by permission of W·W·Norton & Company, Inc.

'Chiseled Clouds,' 'Rosalie,' 'Sight Seed,' 'Significances,' 'Commissary,' 'For Emily Wilson from a Newcomer,' 'Yadkin Picnic,' 'Keeping Track' and 'Alligator Holes down along about Old Dock' reprinted from *The North Carolina Poems* by A.R. Ammons © 1994 by A.R. Ammons

'Making Fields' originally appeared in *Tar River Poetry* © 2009 John R. Ammons

'My father used to tell of an,' 'My father used to bring banana,' 'My father, I hollow for you,' 'I'm the type' and 'When I was young the silk' reprinted from *The Snow Poems* by A.R. Ammons © 1977 by A.R. Ammons, by permission of W·W·Norton & Company, Inc.

'Easter Morning' reprinted from *A Coast of Trees* by A.R. Ammons © 1981 by A.R. Ammons, by permission of W·W·Norton & Company, Inc.

'For My Beloved Son,' 'Broad Brush' and 'Lofty Calling' reprinted from *Brink Road* by A.R. Ammons © 1996 by A.R. Ammons, by permission of W·W·Norton & Company, Inc.

'First Carolina said-song,' 'I broke a sheaf of light,' 'Interval,' 'Help,' 'Nelly Myers,' 'Hardweed path going,' 'Mule Song,' 'Coon Song,' 'Silver,' 'The constant,' 'Definitions,' 'The next day,' 'Trouble making trouble,' 'Motion for motion,' 'Christmas Eve,' 'Second Carolina said-song,' 'The Yucca Moth,' 'Gravelly Run,' 'Cascadilla Falls' and 'Life in the boondocks' reprinted from *Collected Poems, 1951-1971,* by A.R. Ammons © 1972 by A.R. Ammons, by permission of W·W·Norton & Company, Inc.

'Surprising Elements,' 'Body Marks,' 'Dishes and Dashes' and 'Between Each Song' reprinted from *Bosh and Flapdoodle* by A.R. Ammons © 2005 by John R. Ammons, by permission of W·W·Norton & Company, Inc.

'When I was young under the apple' and 'Uncle John Was' reprinted from *Glare* by A.R. Ammons © 1997 by A.R. Ammons, by permission of W·W·Norton & Company, Inc.

'Chinaberry' was originally published in the *Quest* © 1969 by A.R. Ammons

'Making Fields' and 'Chinaberry' are published courtesy of John R. Ammons.

The North Carolina Poems

I WENT BACK

I went back
to my old home
and the furrow
of each year
plowed like
surf across
the place had
not washed
memory away.

FIRST CAROLINA SAID-SONG
(as told me by an aunt)

In them days
    they won't hardly no way to know if
      somebody way off
    died
        till they'd be
        dead and buried

      and Uncle Jim

hitched up a team of mules to the wagon
and he cracked the whip over them
      and run them their dead-level best
the whole thirty miles to your great grandma's funeral
        down there in
          Green Sea County

        and there come up this
awfulest rainstorm
      you ever saw in your whole life
      and your grandpa
      was setting
      in a goat-skin bottomed chair

and them mules a-running
and him sloshing round in that chairful of water

   till he got scalded
   he said

   and ev-
ery
anch of skin come off his behind:

we got there just in time to see her buried
   in an oak grove up
   back of the field

it's growed over with soapbushes and huckleberries now.

CHISELED CLOUDS

A single
cemetery
wipes out
most
of my
people,
skinny old
slabs
leaning this
way
and that
as
in stray
winds,
holding names:

still, enough
silver
cathedrals fill
this
afternoon sky
to
house everyone
ever
lost from
the
light's returning.

I BROKE A SHEAF OF LIGHT

   I broke a sheaf of light
      from a sunbeam
that was slipping through thunderheads
drawing a last vintage from the hills
O golden sheaf I said
and throwing it on my shoulder
brought it home to the corner
   O very pretty light I said
   and went out to my chores
The cow lowed from the pasture and I answered
yes I am late
already the evening star
The pigs heard me coming and squealed
From the stables a neigh reminded me
yes I am late having forgot
I have been out to the sunbeam
and broken a sheaf of gold
     Returning to my corner
I sat by the fire with the sheaf of light
that shone through the night
and was hardly gone when morning came

MY FATHER USED TO TELL OF AN

My father used to tell of an
old lady so old
they ran her down and knocked
her in the head with
a lightered knot
to bury her (then
there was another
one so old
she dried up and turned
to something good to eat)

what my father enjoyed
most—in terms of pure,
high pleasure—was
scaring things: I remember
one day he and
I were coming up in Aunt
Lottie's yard
when there were these
ducks ambling
along in the morning sun,
a few drakes, hens, and a string of
ducklings,
and my father took off his
strawhat and
shot it spinning out sailing in

a fast curving glide over the
ducks so they
thought they were being
swooped by a hawk,
and they just, it looked
like, hunkered down on their
rearends and slid all the
way like they were
greased right under the house
   (in those days houses
   were built up off the ground)
my father laughed the purest,
highest laughter
till he bent over
thinking about those
ducks sliding under
there over nothing

my father, if you could rise
up to where he was at, knew
how to get fun straight
out of things
   he was a legend
   in my lifetime

I remember when he was so
strong he could carry me and
my sister, one leaning to
each shoulder, with our
feet in the big wooden slop bucket:
he died with not a leg
to stand on

yesterday afternoon it snowed &
I scribbled: 'more
uncertain (showery) glory,
flurries and sunshine, the
ground dry because as the
flakes melt on touch the sun
gives the moisture back to
the wind, also uncertain, the
flakes steeply or widely
rising almost as much as
falling but so thin-scattered,
so fine hardly
more than an uninformed
bluster—really nice, the
sun cracking stark bright off
one cloudhead and plunging
paling and dissolving like a
flake into a new blue summit'

today's spanking bright blue
(gold willows and green evergreens)
and chilly, a
little fresh-windy, great day for a walk

INTERVAL

Coming to a pinywoods
    where a stream darted across the path
like a squirrel or frightened blacksnake
I sat down on a sunny hillock
      and leaned back against a pine
and picked up some dry pineneedle bundles from the ground
and tore each bundle apart a needle at a time
  It was not Coulter's pine
  for *coulteri* is funnier looking
  and not Monterey either
and I thought God must have had Linnaeus in mind
orders of trees correspond so well between them
and I dropped to sleep wondering what design God
had meant the human mind to fit
      and looked up and saw a great bird
warming in the sun high on a pine limb
tearing from his breast golden feathers
  softer than new gold that
  dropped to the wind one or two
  gently and touched my face
I picked one up and it said
     The world is bright after rain
for rain washes death out of the land and hides it far
beneath the soil and it returns again cleansed with life
      and so all is a circle
and nothing is separable

Look at this noble pine from which you are
almost indistinguishable it is also sensible
     and cries out when it is felled
and so I said are trees blind and is the earth black to them
Oh if trees are blind
      I do not want to be a tree
A wind rising of *one in time* blowing the feather away
forsaken I woke
and the golden bird had flown away and the sun
had moved the shadows over me so I rose and walked on

FATHER

I dreamed my father flicked
in his grave
then like a fish in water
wrestled with the ground
surfaced and wandered:
I could not find him
through woods, roots, mires
in his bad shape: and
when I found him he was
dead again and had to be
re-entered in the ground:
I said to my mother I still
have you: but out of the
dream I know she died
sixteen years before his
first death:
as I become a child again
a longing that will go away
only with my going grows.

HELP

From the inlet
surf a father
pulls in a crab—
a wonderful machinery
but
not a fish: kicks
it off the line &
up the beach
where three daughters
and two sons take
turns bringing cups
of water
to keep alive, to
watch work, the sanded
& disjeweled.

WHEN I WAS YOUNG UNDER THE APPLE

when I was young under the apple
trees, the very whispering of the

breezes seemed the parental (and
societal) authority: so I became

hooked on the nature of things:
when I learned the breeze and the

repression were not the same, I still
did nothing about it, because it

seemed disrespectful to me to criticize
the creators (after all, they (or

he or it) made the apple trees) so

I went right on thinking myself wrong
(in some ways I was) and the superego

right: I've run around supporting,
literally propping up, my victimizers,

establishing them in praise cubicles
when oopsy-daisy they were as screwed

up as I am and made a mess of creation,
namely, me: Lord, here I am old, and

my life of service has drained me,
and I have worked to earn the respect

of those I no longer respect: have mercy
on me: you cannot, I suppose, give

me another chance: right? well, I
never expected it: but I certainly

do wish I had worked through my
adolescence and kissed the past

goodbye (only to return later free
for a different worship:) I don't

suppose you want to hear anything
more about me today: well, you know

after a hard freeze, say at the end
of November or very early December,

ephemerae and moths bound and flutter
about on a warmish day like posthumous

trash: what do these things mean,
starting so late as ghosts when the

hard water is dripping from its
prophecy of what's to come: dust-winged

soft-flown entities, not a bee-buzz
or mosquito-whine among them, the

living dead or doomed, the mockery of
summer, of fall, already shut down,

the crickets stunned silent where
they stood like little cargoes of

recollection: I don't suppose you
want to hear anymore about bugs:

when I was in the second grade, I
came home one day, and my mother made

me kneel before her aproned knees,
and she ran a fine-tooth comb thru

my hair, and the plump little head
lice dribbled out onto the white

apron: I was looking right at them:
their fine legs wiggled their

relocation about: my itchy scalp
felt so good: my mother scraped away

for days to get the nits: we were
clean people: I caught them boogers

from somebody, but I never did get
the itch, even though a few poor

people came in smelling awful (to
school, I mean) because their parent

had greased them for the itch: one
time a student told the teacher her

mother said 'she warn't greasing
fer the itch till adder Christmas':

it smelt so, I mean: better to scratch
than stink for the holidays, is my

opinion, too: I had a clean pair
of overalls every Monday morning:

that's the way it went

MOTIONING

My father did not
get a resolution
to his problems: he

was taken down
from them: a
vessel broke

in his brain, and
he lost half his
capability: he

walked less and
asked no questions:
sense returned

to his eyes and
with one hand he held
the other

up: that was
stopped when the
central

heart, of which there
is only one,
ticked off: my

father, I could
tell, had
a lot of questions to

ask: but all
motion was
removed from the matter.

MEMORIES, TAPESTRIES

memories, tapestries:
a huge
   wild cherry tree
   grew
   in the bank
   of the old deep ditch
   that cut
   all across the farm
   from road to swamp:
     field-tree, shady
& cool: big roots, turned
gnarled as bark,
stuck out deep down
dark
with damp:
vines o vines
   running here & there all
   over the place tangling—
   jasmine vines or some
kind of honeysuckle
(not the shrub honeysuckle
of open woods)
     but deep down in the
     ditch, crawled into,
     an opening, cool,

vineless,
with somber trickle of
clear water:
that's where I used to
    find the
      diamondback
turtle: yellow stars on
black shell: cool &
        mysterious,
with ruddy-yellow spotted
mouth: a hold of
    wildness
      leaping in the veins—
like a fountain, or,
prolonged, excitement
    moderate & lingering
as a spring
oozing into the ditch:

    a full tree, alone,
that took on space far &
high as it could reach:
  corn wdn't grow
  anywhere around:
  would yellow,
shrivel, never come
to tassel:

  that's why
  one May
  we girdled
    the tree, a narrow

belt of white meat
showing and then
the old heavy branches
lightened
    and all the stiff
      fingers
      pierced black pleas
      into the empty sky:

in my memory all is
white with blossom: the
ground is
purple with
blackcherry stain:
    and green
    leaves hold
way up into the day
an oasis of cool,
   settling air:
   the turtle swims
in my hand:
water nearly declares its
running on:

time so far gone: a
new nakedness
     at the ends of rows:
     a new nakedness
   of need:

how can these
pictures stay
in my head:

  how, after lying 30
yrs in darkness, can
they be brought up,
looked at, and
resubstantiated?
  what we don't
  know's a scare
  & comfort:
how could we react
if we heard the machinery
of our reactions?

 there is a silence
 in us:

     here
     I
     will
     make
     room
     for
     more:

the record the surf leaves
on the shore
 relates tenuously to
 any given wave

 yet is an exact
 history:

                I can't hear
                all the waves
                lapping
            back in my life
                still
                there's a song
running through,
wanting to come out here:

    country darkness:
no street-corner light:
a yellow kerosene
lamp
across the fields, blown
out:
    stars
    in an uncompromised
clarity
rushed into, dusting
    the heavens:
    see that?
    where?
over there—cat-eyes:
    two little stars:
look at that
luminous dust,
the thick axis of the
galaxy:
        on
        this cool
        sandpath
I'm experiencing
the galaxy?

human concern in
country darkness is
    narrow
       & short of range
in a wide
rangeless house!

MAKING FIELDS

My father said the meat came off the insides of his father's hands
said his father working the tar kilns would of a freezing morning
burn his raw hands on the hauling chains,
the chains sticky with cold, I don't know what job my father said
my grandfather was doing, I saw a tar kiln once, though, it was
a burial, fat-lightered slabs laid together in a deep coffin,
buried over, set afire at one end for a muffled burn,
black drops of tar oozing out into a catch basin, I was too young,
maybe I never really saw one but heard of it

also my grandfather (who gave my older sister an apple one day when
she was three, she remembers) got drunk occasionally and, one time,
in Whiteville (then known as Vinland) North Carolina, one
time my grandfather poured a pint down his ox's throat and the fool
ox spun the wheels off the cart leaping and farting the
whole four miles home, my grandfather, they say, meanwhile,
standing in front of the cart and hooting and yelling
round the curves

they say my grandfather was all man, he raised thirteen children on
a small farm he dug out of the woods, he laid out ditches and
fencerows,
he had peacocks, guinea chickens, turkeys, geese, cows, hogs
(the hogs and cows free-ranged, the fields fenced in)

when my father lay with his stroke, I came to sit by him, but
he knew, having sat by his father, too, and stopped eating: dying
fathers despise the solicitude of their sons, death
more rigorous than the wandering eyes of caring, but my father,
they say, was like his father, he could call *leatherbritches*

half an hour away walking home, and my mother would get a tater and a piece of meat ready for him by the time she could see him:

the land is not deep down but across, as into time: the runs, the ditch banks, the underbrush, the open fields with a persimmon tree or wild cherry call, they call me.

MY FATHER USED TO BRING BANANA

My father used to bring banana
stalks home from town
and place them in the chicken coop
so chicken mites would stick
to them
     & a few years ago we had
a flare-up in the local
papers here about feeding layers
crushed oyster shells
to thicken egg shells

forty years ago in Carolina
we used to
bring home a towsack full
of oyster shells every time we went
to the beach

and we had this big old anvil and
big old hammer to
beat up the oyster shells with
     I don't know what became
     of the roosters
     that ate them
     broke out an
     extra set of teeth
my father sure was a mess

this part of my poem is
called chicken (gravy, shit, wing, liver)

sometimes I notice my
shadow and think
there's my father
but I'm fifty now
and it's me

MY FATHER, I HOLLOW FOR YOU

My father, I hollow for you
    in the ditches
O my father, I say,
and when brook light, mirrored,
worms
    against the stone ledges
    I think it an unveiling
or coming loose, unsheathing
of flies
O apparition, I cry,
    you have entered in
    and how may you come
    out again
    your teeth will not
    root
    your eyes cannot
unwrinkle, your handbones
may not quiver and stir
O, my father, I cry,
are you returning:
I breathe and see:
it is not you yet it is you

FOR MY BELOVED SON

The blackberries that ripened
soon after you left are

ripening again and thunderstorms
after the broken-down winter

are rolling through here again:
I keep looking for the season

that will bring you home:
I don't know how many times

I've put in the seed, watered
the plants, counted the blossoms.

EASTER MORNING

I have a life that did not become,
that turned aside and stopped,
astonished:
I hold it in me like a pregnancy or
as on my lap a child
not to grow or grow old but dwell on

it is to his grave I most
frequently return and return
to ask what is wrong, what was
wrong, to see it all by
the light of a different necessity
but the grave will not heal
and the child,
stirring, must share my grave
with me, an old man having
gotten by on what was left

when I go back to my home country in these
fresh far-away days, it's convenient to visit
everybody, aunts and uncles, those who used to say,
look how he's shooting up, and the
trinket aunts who always had a little
something in their pocketbooks, cinnamon bark
or a penny or nickel, and uncles who
were the rumored fathers of cousins
who whispered of them as of great, if
troubled, presences, and school

teachers, just about everybody older
(and some younger) collected in one place
waiting, particularly, but not for
me, mother and father there, too, and others
close, close as burrowing
under skin, all in the graveyard
assembled, done for, the world they
used to wield, have trouble and joy
in, gone

the child in me that could not become
was not ready for others to go,
to go on into change, blessings and
horrors, but stands there by the road
where the mishap occurred, crying out for
help, come and fix this or we
can't get by, but the great ones who
were to return, they could not or did
not hear and went on in a flurry and
now, I say in the graveyard, here
lies the flurry, now it can't come
back with help or helpful asides, now
we all buy the bitter
incompletions, pick up the knots of
horror, silently raving, and go on
crashing into empty ends not
completions, not rondures the fullness
has come into and spent itself from

I stand on the stump
of a child, whether myself
or my little brother who died, and
yell as far as I can, I cannot leave this place, for
for me it is the dearest and the worst,
it is life nearest to life which is
life lost: it is my place where
I must stand and fail,
calling attention with tears
to the branches not lofting
boughs into space, to the barren
air that holds the world that was my world

though the incompletions
(& completions) burn out
standing in the flash high-burn
momentary structure of ash, still it
is a picture book, letter-perfect
Easter morning: I have been for a
walk: the wind is tranquil: the brook
works without flashing in an abundant
tranquility: the birds are lively with
voice: I saw something I had
never seen before: two great birds,
maybe eagles, blackwinged, whitenecked
and -headed, came from the south oaring
the great wings steadily; they went
directly over me, high up, and kept on

due north: but then one bird,
the one behind, veered a little to the
left and the other bird kept on seeming
not to notice for a minute: the first
began to circle as if looking for
something, coasting, resting its wings
on the down side of some of the circles:
the other bird came back and they both
circled, looking perhaps for a draft;
they turned a few more times, possibly
rising—at least, clearly resting—
then flew on falling into distance till
they broke across the local bush and
trees: it was a sight of bountiful
majesty and integrity: the having
patterns and routes, breaking
from them to explore other patterns or
better ways to routes, and then the
return: a dance sacred as the sap in
the trees, permanent in its descriptions
as the ripples round the brook's
ripplestone: fresh as this particular
flood of burn breaking across us now
from the sun.

SURPRISING ELEMENTS

The Ammons women (nine of them, my father's
sisters) were jovial women: well, I guess you

could say that: for them, the distance between
fun tears and tears was a flash of seconds:

Aunt Mitt used to say of some old scraggly man
that he was hopper-behind—hopper behinded?

she meant he was all shoulders (or belly) and
no backseat, just some draggy pants with nothing

back there to fill them out, a hopper, do you
reckon: I doubt she meant he was a hopper,

always looking to hop on something, if you get
my inclination: I think she meant something

to fill up, as in picking green beans in the
field and carrying them in a hopper: Aunt Mitt

died in the front bedroom: the parlor was on
the other side of this long hall: I stood in

line out on Aunt Mitt's porch when I was sixteen
to receive with others her coffin to put in the

hearse: I was a pallbearer: I was sixteen:
what I saw didn't sink in: I was thinking

something else: though I saw (and recall)
everything very clearly: the room she died in

exists nowhere now probably but in my head:
well, there may be one of her seven surviving:

it was a long time ago: I wish I knew: Aunt
Lottie was such an eager woman, so full of

life and laughter: what became of her will
make a short story long.…

NELLY MYERS

    I think of her
        while having a bowl of wheatflakes
(why? we never had wheatflakes
or any cereal then
except breakfast grits)
          and tears come to my eyes
and I think that I will die
because

    the bright, clear days when she was with me
and when we were together
(without caring that we were together)

can never be restored:
        my love wide-ranging
  I mused with clucking hens
and brought in from summer storms
at midnight the thrilled cold chicks
        and dried them out
          at the fireplace
and got up before morning
unbundled them from the piles of rags and
  turned them into the sun:

    I cannot go back
      I cannot be with her again

                    and my love included the bronze
sheaves of broomstraw
she would be coming across the fields with
before the household was more than stirring out to pee

and there she would be coming
    as mysteriously from a new world
and she was already old when I was born but I love
the thought of her hand
wringing the tall tuft of dried grass

        and I cannot see her beat out the fuzzy bloom
again
readying the straw for our brooms at home,
I can never see again the calm sentence of her mind
    as she
measured out brooms for the neighbors and charged
a nickel a broom:

I think of her
    but cannot remember how I thought of her
as I grew up: she was not a member of the family:
I knew she was not my mother,
            not an aunt, there was nothing
visiting about her: she had her room,
    she kept her bag of money
(on lonely Saturday afternoons
    you could sometimes hear the coins
spilling and spilling into her apron):
    she never went away, she was Nelly Myers, we
    called her Nel,

small, thin, her legs wrapped from knees to ankles
in homespun bandages: she always had the soreleg
                       and sometimes
red would show at the knee, or the ankle would swell
and look hot
   (and sometimes the cloths would
dwindle,
       the bandages grow thin, the bowed legs look
pale and dry—I would feel good then,
           maybe for weeks
               there would seem reason of promise,
   though she rarely mentioned her legs
and was rarely asked about them): she always went,

legs red or white, went, went
through the mornings before sunrise
                 covering the fields and
woods
looking for huckleberries
or quieting some wild call to move and go
          roaming the woods and acres of daybreak
and there was always a fire in the stove
when my mother rose (which was not late):

   my grandmother, they say, took her in
when she was a stripling run away from home
(her mind was not perfect
     which is no bar to this love song
            for her smile was sweet,
   her outrage honest and violent)
and they say that after she worked all day her relatives
would throw a handful of dried peas into her lap
                for her supper
and she came to live in the house I was born in the
northwest room of:

oh I will not end my grief
      that she is gone, I will not end my singing;
my songs like blueberries
felt-out and black to her searching fingers before light
welcome her
wherever her thoughts ride with mine, now or in any time
   that may come
when I am gone; I will not end visions of her naked feet
in the sandpaths: I will hear her words
      'Applecandy' which meant Christmas,
'Lambesdamn' which meant Goddamn (she was forthright
     and didn't go to church
  and nobody wondered if she should

and I agree with her the Holcomb pinegrove bordering our
field was
more hushed and lovelier than cathedrals
   not to mention country churches with unpainted boards
and so much innocence as she carried in her face
has entered few churches in one person)

and her exclamation 'Founshy-day!' I know no meaning for
but she knew she was using it right:

and I will not forget how though nearly deaf
she heard the tender blood in lips of children
and knew the hurt
   and knew what to do:

and I will not forget how I saw her last, tied in a chair
lest she rise to go
and fall

           for how innocently indomitable
      was her lust
and how her legs were turgid with still blood as she sat
and how real her tears were as I left
     to go back to college (damn all colleges):
         oh where her partial soul, as others thought,
roams roams my love,
mother, not my mother, grandmother, not my grandmother,
slave to our farm's work, no slave I would not stoop to:
I will not end my grief, earth will not end my grief,
I move on, we move on, some scraps of us together,
   my broken soul leaning toward her to be touched,
listening to be healed.

ROSALIE

My pretty cousin, the hairdresser,
died at thirty, her belly
bigger than a prize pumpkin

but not with anything welcome
on earth: she twisted because
she wanted the thing lifted out

of her, but it was heavier
than she was and more securely
hers than she was the world's:

she said waking up from the shots
the scriptures were
true because she'd just seen

paradise:
I'd ridden my bicycle over to see
her, frogs clunking in along

the brimming ditches by
the pinewoods, green stuff
piling up scumfloats

on the marsh water, and I thought
how fine paradise must be:
for her anything earthless would do.

HARDWEED PATH GOING

       Every evening, down into the hardweed
going,
the slop bucket heavy, held-out, wire handle
freezing in the hand, put it down a minute, the jerky
smooth unspilling levelness of the knees,
       meditation of a bucket rim,
lest the wheat meal,
floating on clear greasewater, spill,
down the grown-up path:

       don't forget to slop the hogs,
       feed the chickens,
       water the mule,
       cut the kindling,
       build the fire,
       call up the cow:

       supper is over, it's starting to get
dark early,
better get the scraps together, mix a little meal in,
nothing but swill.

       The dead-purple woods hover on the west.
I know those woods.
Under the tall, ceiling-solid pines, beyond the edge of
field and brush, where the wild myrtle grows,
       I let my jo-reet loose.

A jo-reet is a bird. Nine weeks of summer he
sat on the well bench in a screened box,
a stick inside to walk on,
  'jo-reet,' he said, 'jo-reet.'
  and I
would come up to the well and draw the bucket down
deep into the cold place where red and white marbled
clay oozed the purest water, water celebrated
throughout the county:
  'Grits all gone?'
  'jo-reet.'
Throw a dipper of cold water on him. Reddish-black flutter.
  'reet, reet, reet!'

  Better turn him loose before
cold weather comes on.
  Doom caving in
  inside
  any pleasure, pure
  attachment
  of love.

Beyond the wild myrtle away from cats I turned him loose
and his eye asked me what to do, where to go;
he hopped around, scratched a little, but looked up at me.
Don't look at me. Winter is coming.
Disappear in the bushes. I'm tired of you and will
be alone hereafter. I will go dry in my well.
  I will turn still.
Go south. Grits is not available in any natural form.
Look under leaves, try mushy logs, the floors of pinywoods.
South into the dominion of bugs.

>   They're good woods.
> But lay me out if a mourning dove far off in the dusky pines
>   starts.
>
>   Down the hardweed path going,
> leaning, balancing, away from the bucket, to
> Sparkle, my favorite hog, sparse, fine black hair,
> grunted while feeding if rubbed,
> scratched against the hair, or if talked to gently:
> got the bottom of the slop bucket:
>   'Sparkle . . .
>   You hungry?
>   Hungry, girly?'
> blowing, bubbling in the trough.
>
>   Waiting for the first freeze:
> 'Think it's going to freeze tonight?' say the neighbors,
> the neighbors, going by.
>
>   Hog-killing.
>
> Oh, Sparkle, when the axe tomorrow morning falls
> and the rush is made to open your throat,
> I will sing, watching dry-eyed as a man, sing my
>   love for you in the tender feedings.
>
>   She's nothing but a hog, boy.
>
> Bleed out, Sparkle, the moon-chilled bleaches
>   of your body hanging upside-down
> hardening through the mind and night of the first freeze.

MULE SONG

Silver will lie where she lies
sun-out, whatever turning the world does,
longeared in her ashen, earless,
floating world:
indifferent to sores and greenage colic,
where oats need not
come to,
bleached by crystals of her trembling time:
beyond all brunt of seasons, blind
forever to all blinds,
inhabited by
brooks still she may wraith over broken
fields after winter
or roll in the rye-green fields:
old mule, no defense but a mule's against
disease, large-ribbed,
flat-toothed, sold to a stranger, shot by a
stranger's hand,
not my hand she nuzzled the seasoning-salt from.

WE LOST OUR MULE KATE

we lost our mule Kate in
the fall
to a chattel mortgage:
   men backed the truck
   up into a shallow
ditch, dropped the ramp,
& with twitch & whip
loaded her on:

it seemed, rather than
   justice,
violation, breakage:
tearing into
a mule's knowledge: &
I stood by, a boy,
violated & hard:

Kate was small, willing
at a touch of straw
to run a wagon harder than
you meant:
   she lunged in the
   high-boarded truck:
her ears flicked, her
eyes set back, blank &

reasonless: she
drowned from herself & us
when the motor, roaring
over all meaning,
tore into gear:

farm with no mule:
the corn she made
    to lie all winter
in a barn's weevil-dust
& rat droppings:

in the spring, a tragic
mule, bony,
    majestical
    came to us:

never forget first time I
saw her, coming down the
Chadbourn road: my
    father went to town
    in the morning:
late that afternoon,
sitting on the washbench,
waiting, I saw him
    coming, new wagon &
new mule:
she seemed hardly to be
walking,
but the legs went out &
out in a reach
    that covered ground:

I called her Silver—O
   loved beast,
   dead & gone,
   not to be lost from mind
   & song—
because
though huge & tired, she
wd rise to her hindlegs
at a touch of heels to
her sides
and run stiff & fast: like
the Lone Ranger's horse:
& Silver was black:
   she possessed the
mark of play,
      a liveliness silly,
inappropriate & great:

SILVER

     I thought Silver must have snaked logs
        when young:
she couldn't stand to have the line brush her lower hind leg:
in blinded halter she couldn't tell what had loosened behind her
        and was coming
as downhill
to rush into her crippling her to the ground:

and when she almost went to sleep, me dreaming at the slow plow,
I would
at dream's end turning over the mind to a new chapter
     let the line drop and touch her leg
     and she would
bring the plow out of the ground with speed but wisely
fall soon again into the slow requirements of our dreams:
how we turned at the ends of rows without sense to new furrows
and went back
     flicked by
     cornblades and hearing the circling in
the cornblades of horseflies in pursuit:

  I hitch up early, the raw spot on Silver's shoulder
sore to the collar,
get a wrench and change the plow's bull-tongue for a sweep,
and go out, wrench in my hip pocket for later adjustments,
     down the ditch-path
by the white-bloomed briars, wet crabgrass, cattails,
       and rusting ferns,

riding the plow handles down,
   keeping the sweep's point from the ground,
the smooth bar under the plow gliding,
the traces loose, the raw spot wearing its soreness out
in the gentle movement to the fields:

      when snake-bitten in the spring pasture grass
Silver came up to the gate and stood head-down enchanted
         in her fate
I found her sorrowful eyes by accident and knew:
nevertheless the doctor could not keep her from all
the consequences, rolls in the sand, the blank extension
         of limbs,
      head thrown back in the dust,
useless unfocusing eyes, belly swollen
wide as I was tall
and I went out in the night and saw her in the solitude
         of her wildness:

but she lived and one day half got up
and looking round at the sober world took me back
         into her eyes
and then got up and walked and plowed again;
mornings her swollen snake-bitten leg wept bright as dew
and dried to streaks of salt leaked white from the hair.

UNCLE JOHN WAS

Uncle John was a cap'm at the beach back when
the world was trying to begin: those old days

yes, sir: he could spot a school from the
shore: the rowboat would drop, and the men

would haul net out 150 yards into the breakers and
circle back, pop out of the boat and pulling

on each end of the arc drag in a furrow of
fish yea high and 100 feet long—spots,

mullet, croakers, crabs, whale shit, and stuff
like you never seen: the men, black, would

divvy up the catch (except the cap'm got more)
and sell what they could and as dusk came

fires along the beach would break out as the
men boiled fish in iron pots and roasted

sweet potatoes: talk about good: talk about
a hongry: all this is a strain in my makeup:

quite a strain: Lord, how I wish I had lived
then, for that! mincing words will not do for

the flap of a fish on the wet sand: something
you caught, something to sell: I went to

grammar school and plowed the fucking clods
instead, a serious person, little given to

human life: Uncle John was later sheriff for
sixteen years and owned a whole beach: he was

feeling good one day (white lightning) and
reached into the back seat of his Terraplane &

gave me twenty dollars, me, just twelve years
old and in love with nothing but paper pads &

PENCILS

I'M THE TYPE

I'm the type
>FARM BOY MAKES GOOD
>>(not farming)

or, with more development tho
still very commonly,
Redneck Kid Grows Up On
Farm Goes Through Depression
But Thanks To Being In
Big War Goes To College
Gets Big Job Making
Big Money
>(relatively speaking)

so that I am not much of a
person after all and
do not need be, the
lineations of the type
include egregious individuality

broaden lineation or
replicate included space

>because of last fall's
>late bloom-thinning
>the forsythia is
>this year not a
>golden bulwark but a
>yellow sprinkle bush

when the wind blows through
my round yew
it changes directions so many
times to get round the branches
and needle leaves
it wears itself out
half way through:
eventually, though, demolished
smooth, really put together,
it floats on through and out,
a massive, indifferent
tranquility available to give
substance to quick turns or
swerves

REDNECK FARM BOY WRITE GOOD
(doesn't sell much)
WRITE VERY GOOD
(but misses
farm, etc., also other rednecks)
MAKE NO MONEY
BUT
WRITE NICE
(tries hard)
(misses the mules and cows,
hogs and chickens, misses
the rain making little
rivers, well-figured with
tributaries, through the
sand yard)

REDNECK UNDERSTAND OTHERS
WRITE A LOT
(books too good
to sell, leave on
shelf in bookstore)

REDNECK START TO SOUND LIKE
INDIAN

him remember Indian burial
mounds in woods, sandy pine woods,
also used to plow up arrowheads
and not think much of it

HIM REDNECK
OPERATE UNDER TOTEM
WASP
(barefoot all summer)
(get hookworm)
(pale neck)

BROAD BRUSH

To the intricacy of the webbing, oh, good,
here comes the broad, coarse, blunt, how
honorable they are, they walk with plunging

casualness, tearing without knowing
through the spun fur of subtlety, and
cyclists put the rubber on the road, turn

around and put down more, see who
can put down most, and the farmer plants
fire wild in the fall field's shifty wind and

breathes the smoke with an assurance of
wine bouquet and another farmer mounts the
combine and eats soybean dust for

hours (the phlegm, he says, digests it and
brings it up again) and good lord what room
the round swearer gives the language, he

surrounds the possibilities of elegance, pours
bad beer into the roundness the words fly out
from: I'm tired of honed lines and high

wires and bickering niceties of balance:
disc up an acre by mistake (it was already
seeded) split the rip saw through two or

three grand poplars (tulip leaf and tulip
cone) and let us kick around unsure
and free, legislation so much milkweed silk.

COON SONG

I got one good look
    in the raccoon's eyes
        when he fell from the tree
came to his feet
    and perfectly still
        seized the baying hounds
in his dull fierce stare,
    in that recognition all
        decision lost,
choice irrelevant, before the
    battle fell
        and the unwinding
of his little knot of time began:

        Dostoevsky would think
it important if the coon
    could choose to
        be back up the tree:
or if he could choose to be
    wagging by a swamp pond,
        dabbling at scuttling
crawdads: the coon may have
    dreamed in fact of curling
        into the holed-out gall
of a fallen oak some squirrel
    had once brought
        high into the air
clean leaves to: but

                reality can go to hell
is what the coon's eyes said to me:
        and said how simple
                the solution to my
problem is: it needs only
        not to be: I thought the raccoon
                felt no anger,
saw none; cared nothing for cowardice,
        bravery; was in fact
                bored at
knowing what would ensue:
        the unwinding, the whirling growls,
                exposed tenders,
the wet teeth—a problem to be
        solved, the taut-coiled vigor
                of the hunt
ready to snap loose:

                you want to know what happened,
you want to hear me describe it,
        to placate the hound's-mouth
                slobbering in your own heart:
I will not tell you: actually the coon
        possessing secret knowledge
                pawed dust on the dogs
and they disappeared, yapping into
        nothingness, and the coon went
                down to the pond
and washed his face and hands and beheld
        the world: maybe he didn't:
                I am no slave that I
should entertain you, say what you want
        to hear, let you wallow in
                your silt: one two three four five:
one two three four five six seven eight nine ten:

        (all this time I've been
            counting spaces
while you were thinking of something else)
        mess in your own sloppy silt:
            the hounds disappeared
yelping (the way you would at extinction)
        into — the order
        breaks up here — immortality:
I know that's where you think the brave
        little victims should go:
            I do not care what
you think: I do not care what you think:
        I do not care what you
            think: one two three four five
six seven eight nine ten: here we go
        round the here-we-go-round, the
            here-we-go-round, the here-we-
go-round: coon will end in disorder at the
        teeth of hounds: the situation
            will get him:
spheres roll, cubes stay put: now there
        one two three four five
            are two philosophies:
here we go round the mouth-wet of hounds:

        what I choose
        is youse:
        baby

MEDICINE FOR TIGHT SPOTS

Consider big-city
tensions
rurally unwound,

high-tension lines that
loft through the countryside,
give off

'wirelings'
and fire-up to houses
cool as a single volt:

there are so many ways to approach the problems:
reproach:
best of all the by-pass and set-aside: the

intelligence has never been called for
because as usually
manifested it's

too formulated to swim
unformulable reality's
fall-out insistences:

just think how woodsy roads
shade spangled
wind up big-city printed circuits:

if the mind becomes what it sees or
makes how it works
I know which way I'm headed:

won't bushes bust us
mild:
won't the streams

ravel us loose:
won't we be untold
by sweetwater tongues.

BODY MARKS

Nailing down the cause of anything is not easy:
you notice a prominent strand in the random

weave and think, well, that's probably it: but
that may be there just to mislead the born or

else it works only in association with a set
of subsets or sublineations and only expensive

time can rectify a balance out of that: I say
why is my hipbone flashing out each step down

my femur this morning when I walked less than
usual yesterday: well, too many stairs: well,

slept on that side all night: well, it's really
your colon hurting: what? well, remember

last night during that TV drama you had one
leg stretched out to the coffeetable too long:

that could have defined a warp in your bone
pain calls attention to: well, well: you've

(I've) probably hit on it: which would prove
it out this evening, hanging your leg up there

again or not: that is the question: when in
the second grade, cut on the playground, I,

playing hounds and fox (I was the fox, the slow
boys the hounds) skidded my left knee over the

spike of a buried stump, I got a 3 to 4 inch
slash and nearly passed out: I felt so

important, though: imagine being taken to a
doctor's office! and all the expensive stuff

was unwound and wound onto me, with taping
and splinting (I almost said splintering):

3 weeks off from school: stitches put in,
torn out by bending the knee, re-stitched, and

you know how it goes when you're eight: I'm
70 now, and I still can see the little white

raisures where the stitches ripped free: you
could know me anywhere: talk about identity:

I'm nobody else except myself, unless somebody
has a mark just like mine (backed up by

another scar (I won't tell you about now) on
the inside of my left wrist, not an attempt

at anything self-critical:) I'm sure you think
all this is just as important and worthy of

posterity as I do....

THE CONSTANT

When leaving the primrose, bayberry dunes, seaward
I discovered the universe this morning,
        I was in no
mood
for wonder,
    the naked mass of so much miracle
already beyond the vision
of my grasp:

along a rise of beach, a hundred feet from the surf,
a row of clam shells
    four to ten feet wide
    lay sinuous as far as sight:

in one shell—though in the abundance
        there were others like it—upturned,
four or five inches across the wing,
a lake
three to four inches long and two inches wide,
all dimensions rounded,
    indescribable in curve:

and on the lake a turning galaxy, a film of sand,
co-ordinated, nearly circular (no real perfections),
    an inch in diameter, turning:
turning:
counterclockwise, the wind hardly perceptible from 11 o'clock
      with noon at sea:

        the galaxy rotating,
        but also,
at a distance from the shell lip,
revolving
round and round the shell:

       a gull's toe could spill the universe:
two more hours of sun could dry it up:
a higher wind could rock it out:

the tide will rise, engulf it, wash it loose:
utterly:

the terns, distressed to see me there, their
    young somewhere hidden in clumps of grass or weed,
were diving *sshik sshik* at me,
       then pealing upward for another round and dive:

I have had too much of this inexhaustible miracle:
miracle, this massive, drab constant of experience.

DEFINITIONS

The weed bends
  down and
becomes a bird:
the bird
  flies white

through winter
  storms: I
have got my
interest up in
  leaf

transparencies:
  where I am
going, nothing
of me will remain:
  yet, I'll

drift through the
  voices of
coyotes, drip
into florets by
  a mountain rock.

TRANSFER

When the bee lands the
morning glory bloom
dips some and weaves:
  the coming true of
  weight
  from weightless wing-held
  air
  seems at the touch
  implausible.

THE NEXT DAY

Morning glory vine
slight
as it is will
double on itself and
pile over
a quince bush before
you know it:
so the woodless-stemmed
can
by slender travel
arrange its leaves and
take away
light from the wooded:
beholding the rampancy
and the
thin-leaved quince
thereunder, I stripped
off an armload
of vine
and took it down to
the brushheap
under the pear tree:
the next day
the wilted leaves had
given up their
moisture to the
vines that here and
there
to diminished glory
lifted half-opened
morning glory blooms.

THE QUINCE BUSH

The flowering quince bush
on the back hedge has been
run through by a morning
glory vine

and this morning three blooms
are open as if for all light,
sound, and motion: their adjustment
to light is

pink, though they reach for
stellar reds and core violets:
they listen as if for racket's
inner silence

and focus, as if to starve, all motion:
patterns of escaped sea
they tip the defeated, hostile,
oceanic wind:

elsewhere young men scratch and fire:
a troubled child shudders to a freeze:
an old man bursts finally and
rattles down

clacking slats: the caterpillar pierced
by a wasp egg blooms inside with
the tender worm: wailing
walls float

luminous with the charge of grief:
a day pours through a morning glory
dayblossom's adequate, poised,
available center.

LOFTY CALLING

Chimney-top, aerial- or cherry-tree-top,
Bob Shorter's mockingbird
splits daybreak to air-light glint glass,
chips slabs superfine, bubbles and pops

blisters, chisels light to pane-flint floats:
he wangles crescendos up from
cedar roots and sprays improvisations
into as many song-tips as cedar tips;

then with stark repetition
hacks a few cedars down:
he works at it—air's tilled over Bob's
place, tone-farmed: and then

at times, as if restless with stodgy air,
Shorter's mockingbird gets
the leaps and leaps on song swells
and settles down again as if into

buoys of his own music:
line and formation apprise the air;
invention on invention piled up
figure the invisible invisibly.

SIGHT SEED

When the jay caught
the cicada midair, a fluffy,
rustling beakful, the
burr-song flooded dull but
held low: the jay perched and
holding the prey to the branch
as if to halt
indecorous song pecked
once, a plink that did it,
but in the noticeable silence
proceeded at ease
and expertly to
take this, then that eye.

TROUBLE MAKING TROUBLE

The hornet as if
stung twists
in the first cold,
buzzes wings

that wrench him
across the ground but
take on no
loft or

direction:
scrapes with feelers
his eyes to find
clearance

in the crazing
dim of things, folds
to bite his tail (or
sting his

head) to life or
death—hits the
grill of a stormdrain
and drops.

GOT TO LEAVE

   got
      to leave Sissy Fuss
      & go
      pick out the Christmas
      tree:
      keep it cold in
      garage: so it don't
turn stiff & sheddy:
      cut'em around October:
      why
      they cut'em so soon?
      transportation:
      it's mechandising:
dealerships to work out:
farmers to contact: red
      tape: whatd'ya
think?
they can just appear up
down here
fresh
two days before Christmas?
sheez!
some kindova nut:

    grows on a tree,
    a tree is part of
      Nature,

Nature is beautiful &
thank you for the
          compliment:

why don't we go cut
our own?
cut our own?
where?
but we don't own that land:
whatd'ya mean they don't
care?
I know they're beautiful
grow right up in the
fallow land,
    taper up nice, standing
out half-deep in
    Indian grass, right
out in the middle of
    the field:

when I was a boy:
or a bit more:
used to go get the
    Christmas tree: lived
way out in the country
down in Carolina
in a time
& place
that seem so long ago,
everything different
now and sort of loused up:

an only boy & I would get
the axe &
follow the paths over the
fields & back of the
    fields come into
hill-woods (hickory,

  lush-leaved tree,
   covering the ground each
year with
thick-shelled nuts)
& then into the swamp woods:
  for
in the South
cedar grows deep
  in the damp swampwoods
and then it's sparse, so
sparse, where I come from:
& walk & walk, roaming and
nearly lost:
there's one! already
  topped: and found
another, shaggy, topped
years ago: & finally
finally finding one
   bushy, full, &
   pointed:
climbing and with that
awkward, ungrounded swing,
hacking away at the
  trunk:
dragging it home, the limbs
obliging, flowing with
the motion:

we had no electricity but
we had pinecones &
  colored paper &
  some tinsel: it
was beautiful enough:
it was very lovely:
& it's lost:

though there's no
        returning (and
shd be little desire
to return) still we shd
keep the threads looped
tightly with past years,
the fabric
taut
& continuous, past growing
into present so present
can point to future:

where am I now?
in a house with
no acres around it—don't
        even own an axe—
plenty of electricity but
no hickory nuts,
no rumaging the swamp
for the scented green,
the green-green, moist,
growing right on the tree:
now, a tree from
somewhere—maybe Vermont—
got by handing over
    two or three green
    pcs of paper:
        $$$$$$$$$$$$

CHRISTMAS EVE

When cold, I huddle up, foetal, cross
arms:
but in summer, sprawl:

   secret is plain old
surface area,
decreased in winter, retaining: in summer no
     limbs touching—
radiating:
everything is physical:

     chemistry is physical:
     electrical noumenal mind
  is:
(I declare!)

put up Christmas tree this afternoon:
     fell
asleep in big chair: woke up at
3:12 and it
   was snowing outside, was white!

Christmas Eve tonight: Joseph
is looking for a place:
Mary smiles but
     her blood is singing:

      she will have to lie down:
     hay is warm:
some inns keep only
the public room warm: Mary

is thinking, Nice time
      to lie down,
good time to be brought down by this necessity:

I better get busy
and put the lights on — can't find
   extension cord:
Phyllis will be home, will say, The
tree doesn't have any lights!
I have tiny winking lights, too:
      she will like
them: she went to see her mother:

my mother is dead: she is
deep in the ground, changed: if she
rises, dust will blow all over the place and
   she will stand there shining,
smiling: she will feel good:
she will want
to go home and fix supper: first she
     will hug me:

an actual womb bore Christ,
divinity into the world:
   I hope there are births to lie down to
back
to divinity,
since we all must die away from here:

I better look for the cord:
we're going to
      the Plaza for dinner:
tonight, a buffet: tomorrow there, we'll
   have a big Christmas
dinner:

before I fell asleep, somebody
phoned, a Mr. Powell: he asked
      if I wanted to
sell my land
in Mays Landing: I don't know:
I have several pieces, wonder
   if he wants them all,
wonder what I ought to quote:

earth: so many acres of earth:
own:
how we own who are owned! well,
anyway, he won't care
      about that—said he would
call back Monday: I will
tell him something then:
   it's nearly Christmas, now:
they are all going into the city:
some have sent ahead for reservations:
the inns are filling up:

      Christ was born
in a hay barn among the warm cows and the
donkeys kneeling down: with Him divinity
swept into the flesh
   and made it real.

TODAY IS DIM AGAIN

28 Dec:

today
is dim
again:

the sun makes diffuse
shadows
that go
in & out
of focus:

      (just now, the
  thorns
  are black
  against the wall)

maybe it's gonna clear off:
not very cold:

there comes the exactness
again:
pulsing:

gaits:
short/quick-stepping Kate:
Silver,
  long & languorous:
  what

to do in case of fall-out
put it
back in & use
   shorter strokes:

   brushstrokes:
   short, straight, narrow
strokes
that blend & move
   into vague scenes:
   the broad, long
swash of color:

   the paroxysmic:
   the full, slow
inner & outer reach:

   wavelengths:
   distance, elapse of time
from crest to crest, from
point of highest
   stirred feeling
to highest point: the
   silky, fiery
considerations
   down the hills
   and shallows and up
   the rises
     of repeating motions:

rhythm, pace:
Silver, majestical,
  slow but sure: the
  turn-plow
  turned earth
  to overturning rivers:
smooth, rockless,
alluvial country,
  free of stumps:

  stump-holes, tho—still
in the pasture: the
  hollow shells—inside
  the crater lake
  of ancient wood-ambered
rain, wriggling larvae,
hanging head-down from
  the surface,
  breathing through
their tails, & tiny green
frogs
hidden in crevices
over canyons of wood:
  the thick, grazed
carpet grass
smooth in patches
  around inedible
  wire-grass clumps:
worlds:

the only longleaf pine
left
stood tall & spare-boughed
as land-corner:
    marker between
neighbor & us:
mystical tree:
    half ours,
half his, neither
able to take his half
    without loss of all

    & in addition
transfigured by
    boundary-meaning,
    entered in the record
      (history in the
courthouse)
a sign:

spared: let us take on
  meanings to
  keep us:

  standing alone in the
  edge of the pasture,
near the road
(the road when it came
  through
  cut off a sliver of the
neighbor's land

so it was worthless to
   him—our pasture
   fence included his
   sliver &
the tree stood in from the
road—is the way it really
   was: and the road &
tree became symbols
of two kinds of truth,
competing:
            the tree, ideals of
            truth:
            the road, the use of
            this world
& compromise)
            high sparse
            branches
            sang
            thin songs:
            (one of my uncles, I
heard said, used to
go into the woods to pray,
always to a
   particular tree:
   a praying tree—
   must have had
   meanings
   in it)

if you don't think
mechanisms work
  in the green
  becoming
  of
  the
  lichen, I don't care
what you think: it's
one-sided
unaware that
    crystals, even,
    exist
    as fluids:

    thallopyte & green
    alga
    living together,
    with
    necessary exchanges:

    abstractions may
    sight far
    over the facts
    & fall
    short or broken
but meantime it shows
saliences of going:
  its spare thin
  beauty
  is relating:

    reason & feeling
    living together, with
    necessary exchanges:

guidelines—but readiness
to adjust
    to changed
    environments:

what is it that persists
through generations,
    throwing its pattern
    ahead?

MOTION FOR MOTION

Watched on the sandy, stony bottom of the stream
the oval black shadow of the waterbeetle, shadow

larger than beetle, though no blacker, mirroring
at a down and off angle motion for motion, whirl, run:

>   (if I knew the diameters
>   of oval and beetle, the
>   depth of the stream, several
>   indices of refraction
>   and so forth

>   I might say why
the shadow outsizes the
beetle—

I admit to mystery
in the obvious—

but now that I remember some
I think the shadow
included the bent water where
the beetle rode, surface

tension, not breaking, bending
under to hold him up,

the deformation recorded in shade:
for light, arising from so far away,

    is parallel
    through a foot of water
    (though edge-light
    would

    make a difference—a beetle can
    exist among such differences
    and do well):

    someone has a clear vision of it all,
    exact to complete existence;
    loves me when I swear and praise
    and smiles, probably, to see me
    wrestle with sight

    and gain no reason from it, or money,
    but a blurred mind overexposed):

caught the sudden gust of a catbird, selfshot
under the bridge and out into my sight: he splashed
into the air near a briervine, lit:

I don't know by what will: it was clear sailing
on down the stream
and prettier—a moss-bright island made two streams
and then made one and, farther, two fine birches
and a lot of things to see: but he stopped

back to me,
didn't see me, hopped on through the vines, by some
will not including me…

and then there were two beetles, and later three at
once swimming in the sun, and three shadows,
all reproduced, multiplied without effort
or sound, the unique beetle—and I—lost to an

automatic machinery in things, duplicating, without
useful difference, some changeless order extending
backward beyond the origin of earth,

changeless and true, even before the water fell, or
the sun broke, or the beetle turned, or the still
human head bent from a bridge-rail above to have a look.

RECORDING

I remember when freezing
rain bent the yearling
pine over and stuck its
crown to ground ice:
but now it's spring
and the pine stands
up straight, frisky in
the breeze, except for
memory, a little lean.

COMMISSARY

What sort of person in
drought puts a saucer of water out
for hornets: maybe
their placid pulsing
at drink
allures and dreams him:
maybe he needs to appease bees, too,

or wasps or
those glimmery little fellows
too small to name:
or he's seen a hornet
snip a silk-hung worm
from the air under a bough
and liked the address:

I'd as lief
watch a day lily sway:
I don't have a thing for
porcelain or stings:
but it's okay with me:
anything you starve is food,
anything you feed kills.

SECOND CAROLINA SAID-SONG

*(as told me by a patient, Ward 3-B,
Veterans Hospital, Fayetteville, August 1962)*

    I was walking down by the old
Santee
      River
        one evening, foredark
        fishing I reckon,

    when I come on this
swarm of
bees
   lit in the fork of a beech limb
     and they werz

    jest a swarming:

 it was too late to go home
 and too far
and brang a bee-gum

     so I waited around
   till the sun went
down,
most dark,

     and cut me off a pinebough,
     dipped it in the river
       and sprankled water

on 'em: settled 'em right down,
    good and solid,
about
        a bushel of
        them:

        when it got dark I first cut off
the fork branches and
then cut about four foot back toward
        the trunk

and I
        throwed the limb over my shoulder and
            carried 'em home.

THE YUCCA MOTH

    The yucca clump
is blooming,
    tall sturdy spears
spangling into bells of light,
    green
in the white blooms
    faint as a memory of mint:

I raid
    a bloom,
spread the hung petals out,
    and, surprised he is not
a bloom-part, find
    a moth inside, the exact color,
the bloom his daylight port or cove:

though time comes
    and goes and troubles
are unlessened,
    the yucca is lifting temples
of bloom: from the night
    of our dark flights, can
we go in to heal, live
    out in white-green shade
the radiant, white, hanging day?

SIGNIFICANCES

After brief heavy
rain at two o'clock,
he listened at
the wood's edge
and could tell by
the clusters and sheets of drops
that some drops, summarizing
the leaves they'd
fallen from,
were larger than
others or had
fallen farther,
and when the wind waved
wide like a conductor,
a rustle of events,
cool, keyless, spilled:
he listened,
his body sweetened level to
the variable nothingness.

MEDIATION

The grove kept us dry
subtracting from
the shower much
immediacy:

but then distracted us
for hours, dropping
snaps faint as the twigs
of someone coming.

FOR EMILY WILSON FROM A NEWCOMER

When it gets hot here it's really noticeable:
clumps of copperheads unwind,
brotherly younglings, and form separate

rings of attention: maypop blossoms
stretch wide open, nearly closing back on
themselves: black widows, keyed up,

traipse their mates off to dinner:
squirrels sail onto branches tailbone
fine and, swaying, hull nuts: joe-pye

two-men tall on the creek banks blooms,
bonnets as pink and wide as parasols: but
Emily spells welcome warmer than any weather.

GRAVELLY RUN

I don't know somehow it seems sufficient
to see and hear whatever coming and going is,
losing the self to the victory
   of stones and trees,
of bending sandpit lakes, crescent
round groves of dwarf pine:

for it is not so much to know the self
as to know it as it is known
   by galaxy and cedar cone,
as if birth had never found it
and death could never end it:

the swamp's slow water comes
down Gravelly Run fanning the long
   stone-held algal
hair and narrowing roils between
the shoulders of the highway bridge:

holly grows on the banks in the woods there,
and the cedars' gothic-clustered
   spires could make
green religion in winter bones:

so I look and reflect, but the air's glass
jail seals each thing in its entity:

no use to make any philosophies here:
   I see no
god in the holly, hear no song from
the snowbroken weeds: Hegel is not the winter
yellow in the pines: the sunlight has never
heard of trees: surrendered self among
   unwelcoming forms: stranger,
hoist your burdens, get on down the road.

YADKIN PICNIC
for Jane and Pat Kelly

It takes so long to set up the terminological landscape,
a rise of assimilation here, wooded underpinnings
fringed by thickets of possibility there, and throughout

in a slope, an undulation falling away to one side, an
old river's work—before one can say, 'May we sweetly
kiss' or 'Mark, the woodlark'—: begins with an airy

nothingness lofted, on one arc of which is a great sea and in
the middle of the sea an island, in the middle of which
a city, and mid-city a spire, the coming to point

of the tallest assumption: after this, it follows
naturally to say. 'Yesterday, after the morning clouds, we
packed lunch and went over to picnic in Aunt Polly's orchard.'

CASCADILLA FALLS

I went down by Cascadilla
Falls this
evening, the
stream below the falls,
and picked up a
handsized stone
kidney-shaped, testicular, and

thought all its motions into it,
the 800 mph earth spin,
the 190-million-mile yearly
displacement around the sun,
the overriding
grand
haul

of the galaxy with the 30,000
mph of where
the sun's going:
thought all the interweaving
motions
into myself: dropped

the stone to dead rest:
the stream from other motions
broke
rushing over it:
shelterless,
I turned

to the sky and stood still:
Oh
I do
not know where I am going
that I can live my life
by this single creek.

DISHES AND DASHES

I always wanted (when I was a boy—and even
now) to have a stretch of water, at least a

farm pond or house pond, a little circular
flat thing with fish in it, pike and bream,

sunflowers: something glassy as the sky, that
could fill up with clouds (cloud and could)

that would crash into the banks where among the
sedges and grasses mosquito hawks and dragonflies

would pitch and tilt: the sheen and silver,
the stillness, a patch of lilies maybe, or a

clutch of cattails a redwing might get close
enough to jeer in: but I still have the sky,

deeper than any stillness I could get water to
hold, and the years go by and it clears blue

and breezy: the geese seesaw back and forth,
talking through: (neither a sayer nor a doer

be: be a beer (nonalcoholic)): much of my
sin is not original: a little verbal abuse

(herein demonstrated), a little self-abuse
(which I make a practice of keeping to myself):

a few painful exaggerations and oversights
(lies), etc., a fairly normal menu: more

nearly original are things like being part of
the web of human relations, wherein, for

example, we used to be tobacco growers, and
my mother, a religious person, hated tobacco

anyhow, but it would have killed her to know
she was killing people, something not known

way back then: but I, I brought the green
leaves up from the field by a Silver-drawn

sled, poor mule: but lately I advised a man
to stop smoking, *and he did,* but he gained

twenty pounds and ran into diabetes and high
blood pressure: put that in your pipe and

—no, no: that's what I mean: get down
on your knees and ask to be excused because

there isn't a damn thing you can do about much
of the damage you do: pray, brother, pray,

and join the praying crowd....

KEEPING TRACK

It's not going to be again the way it was:
Silver won't come up from the pasture again

and stand, head low, dozing by the gate:
the sow won't strike mouthfuls of wiregrass

all day for a rushed bed to farrow in:
I won't ever again hear my father at dusk

holler *leatherbritches* from the woodsroad
coming home or feel the start that things might

once be all right: the plank fence of the barnyard
is down and gone, cornerposts rotted holes:

when my memory goes, my father's never adzed
and mauled those boards from swamp-cut logs.

BETWEEN EACH SONG

I once would have said my sister Vida but now
I can just say my sister because the other

sister is gone: you didn't know Mona, lovely
and marvelous Mona, so you can't feel the

flooded solar plexus that grips me now: but
you may know (I don't know if I hope you will

or hope you won't—tossups between having and
holding) but you may know someone of your own

I don't quite know the pang for as you do: I
know but don't believe Mona is gone: she is

still so much with me, I can hardly tell I lost
anything when I lost so much: love is a very

strange winding about when it gets lost in
your body and especially when it can't find

the place to go to, the place it used to find: Mona is
in my heart in a way that burns my chest until

my eyes water: are you that way: even in the
midst of business I could think of caring for

you for that: but my sister Vida and I used
to have to daub (we called it dob) the baccer

barn: cracks between the uneven-log sides
had to be filled airtight with clay so the

furnace and flues could 'cure' the tobacco
with slow, then high heat: we would dig a

bucket of clay from the ditch by the road
where streaks of white and red clay ran, add

water for a thick consistency, then climb the
rafters inside the barn and dob the cracks:

can you imagine: kids: (perhaps it beat
empty streets filled with drugs): **I REALLY**

THINK WE SHOULD GET IT OFF OR GET OFF IT

WHAT ARE WE TO THINK

What are we to think of the waste, though: the
sugarmaple seeds on the blacktop are so dense,

the seedheads crushed by tires, the wings stuck
wet, they hold the rains, so there's no walkway

dry: so many seeds, and not one will make a
tree, excuse the expression: what of so much

possibility, all impossibility: how about the
one who finds alcohol at eleven, drugs at seventeen

death at thirty-two: how about the little
boy on the street who with puffy-smooth face and

slit eyes reaches up to you for a handshake:
supposing politics swings back like a breeze and

sails tanks through a young crowd: what about the
hopes withered up in screams like crops in

sandy winds: how about the letting out of streams
of blood where rain might have sprinkled into

roadpools: are we to identify with the fortunate
who see the energy of possibility as its necessary

brush with impossibility: who define meaning
only in the blasted landfalls of no meaning:

who can in safety call evil essential to the
differentiations of good: or should we wail

that the lost are lost, that nothing can be right
until they no longer lose themselves, until we've found

charms to call them back: are we to take no
comfort when so much discomfort turns here and

there helplessly for help: is there, in other
words, after the balances are toted up, is there

a streak of light defining the cutting edge as
celebration: (clematis which looks as dead and

drained in winter as baling wire transports in
spring such leaves and plush blooms!) I walked

down the hall to the ward-wing surrounded on
three sides with windows' light and there with

the other diabetics like minnows in the pool-
head of a tidal rising sat my father slumped,

gussied up with straps, in a wheelchair, a catheter leading
to the little fuel tank hung underneath, urine

the color of gasoline, my father like the
others drawn down half-asleep mulling over his

wheels: where, I thought, hope of good is gone
evil becomes the deliverer, and more evil, to get

one through to the clearing where presence, now
pain, enters oblivion: my father roused himself

and took some hope in me but then left me back
alone: at a point in evil, evil changes its

clothes and death with a soft smile crooks its
finger to us: a taking by death leaving the

living bereft: such a mixture! where does a steady
formulation settle down: what integration

of wisdom holds scoured by the bottoms of…
bottoms?…questioned, I mean, by nibbling

exception and branching direction: every balance
overbalances: judiciousness loses the excitement

of error: realizing that there is no safety
is safety: the other side of anything is worth

nearly as much as the side: the difference
so slight in fact, that one goes out to see if

it is there: I want a curvature like the
arising of a spherical section, a sweep that

doesn't break down from arc into word, image,
definition, story, thesis, but all these

assimilated to an arch of silence, an interrelation
permitting motion in stillness: I want to see

furrows of definition, both the centerings of
furrow and the clumpy outcastings beyond: I do

not want to be caught inside for clarity: I
want clarity to be a smooth long bend

disallowing no complexity in coming clean: why
do I want this, complexity without confusion,

clarity without confinement, time in time, not
time splintered: if you are not gone at a certain

age, your world is: or it is shriveled to a
few people who know what you know: aunts and

uncles with their histories blanked out, the thick
tissue of relationships erased into one of emptiness

or maybe your cousins, too, are gone, and
the world has starved to a single peak,

you and what you know alone, with no one
else in the world to nod recognizing what you

say and recall without explanation: so, have
your choice to leave the world or have it leave

you; either way you choose will bring the same
result, nothingness and the vanishment of

what was: over and over the world rolls in this
wise, so much so that people stricken with these

knowledges think the aspiration to win to be
remembered, to be let hanging, dibbling in the

minds of those continuing: but life is not first
for being remembered but for being lived! how

quaint and sad the lives of those who have lived
but are gone, the vacant sadness of two eternities

pressed together, squeezing them dry to
nondegradable remnants—trash: the meaning,

the tears, loves, sweet handholdings, all
the fears, jealousies, hangings, burnings—

throwaways, obsolescences that plug up
the circulations today, burdening the living

with guilty obligations of memory and services:
to have the curvature, though, one needs the

concisions of the local, contemplations such as
how to slice a banana for breakfast oatmeal,

fourteen thick or thirty-three thin events, the
chunky substance of fourteen encounters or the

flavor availabilities in limp circles: fly the
definite lest it lock you in! have solvent by

should the imperative devise you a vice: see
a spread of possibilities, not an onion plot:

the juggler has twice as many balls as hands
because it's all up in the air: keep it up

in the air, boundingly like ephemera at dusk:
or dawn: I saw in Carolina morning flies

midair like floating stones: the dew, heavy;
the sun, blood red: a road dipping round a

pine grove down a hill to a pond, the spillway
clogged with cattails bent with breezes and with

redwings awilding day: a crippled old farmer
up early with his dog, noon likely to melt tar,

a benchlong of old blacks at the crossroads
gas station, dogfennel high on the woods' edge,

some scraggly roastnear corn used up, tomato
plants sprawled out, become vines: morning,

gentlemen, how you all doing: these bitty
events, near pangs commonplace on this planet

so strangely turned out, we mustn't take on so
but let the music sway, the rhetoric ride, the

garbage heave, for if we allow one solid cast
of grief to flip and filter away into all the

trinklets it might go, we would be averaged
down to a multiple diminishment like acceptance:

but we mean to go on and go on till we unwind
the winding of our longset road, when, we

presume, the nothingness we
step to will mirror treasures we leave, a

strange mirror, everything in our lives having
taken root in love, the sequences having become

right because that is the way they had to run:
but, then, for the trouble of love, we may be

so tired that indifference will join ours to the
hills' indifference and the broad currents of

the deep and the high windings of the sky, and
we may indeed see the ease beyond our

understanding because, till now, always beyond

LIFE IN THE BOONDOCKS

Untouched grandeur in the hinterlands:
large-lobed ladies laughing in brook
water, a clear, scrubbed ruddiness lofted

to cones and conifers: frost blurs
the morning elk there and squirrels
chitter with the dawn, numb seed: clarity,

the eagle dips into scary nothingness,
off a bluff over canyon heights: trout
plunder their way up, thrashing the shallows

white: ladies come out in the gold-true sun
and loll easy as white boulders
in the immediate radiance by wind-chilling

streams: I have been there so
often, so often and held the women, squeezed,
tickled, nuzzled their rose-paint luxury:

so many afternoons listened to the rocky
drone of bees over spring-water weed-bloom,
snow-water violets, and distant moss turf.

ALLIGATOR HOLES
DOWN ALONG ABOUT OLD DOCK

Lord, I wish I were in Hallsboro, over by the tracks,
or somewhere down past the Green Swamp around Nakina, or
traipsing, dabbling in the slipping laps of Lake Waccamaw:

how I wish I were over by Fair
Bluff where the old Lumber River snakes under overhanging
cypress-moss, black glass going

gleamy deep and slow, 'gator easy and slow:
I bet a mockingbird's cutting loose a Dido in wisteria
vine or mimosa bush over there right now: if I were

down by Shalotte, the fish fries, scrubby sand-woods,
the beach dunes nearby: or Gause's Landing:
Lord, I wish I were home—those pastures—where I'll

never be again: Spring Branch Church, South
Whiteville, New Brunswick: mother and father, aunts,
uncles gone over, no one coming back again.

WHEN I WAS YOUNG THE SILK

When I was young the silk
of my mind
hard as a peony head
unfurled
and wind bloomed the parachute

The air-head tugged me
up,
tore my roots loose and drove
high, so high

I want to touch down now
and taste the ground
I want to take in
my silk
and ask where I am
before it is too late to know

CHINABERRY

Out in the edge of the yard at evening
under the reaching chinaberry tree
in the belled, gray country silence
mother and father
sitting in the cool on the washbench
the black iron washpot
three-legged and belly burnt
the other side of the path circling the yard,
under the outer arms of the chinaberry umbrella,
the wooden wide bench, soapslick dry,
galvanized tubs upside down,
cold to touch in the summer dusk,
contained, exact inner dreams—
we stand in our diagonal of height,
Mona singing her clear, gospel-singing, happy soprano,
devotional gems, songs of deliverance, glory
trains and royal telephones,
Vida, her thin-faced pale alto self-taught
coming like whippoorwills weary with sleep, next
in height, and I, shortest,
too young to more than keep the tune,
singing together, together to the sandhill fields,
to whatever moves in with night over the pines,
coming from where in the west the far great
cherry on the ditchbank stands, standing out black
against the farther, lower pines,
together to the tired, song-starved mother,
My Friend is the King
to the father of three, three gray faces under

the darkening tree, three here, three in graves,
together to the sleeping coops and quiet barns
Oh where is my wandering boy tonight?
On the top of Mt. Zion is a City
three singing in the deep-lying Carolina country
far from town
'prettiest thing I ever heard'
eyes lost in the green blood of night's tears
of old inherited sorrows, grainy & wasted as the land,
beautiful, wasted as the years in
the mother's face, in the father's hands.

AFTERWORD

Although defining an A. R. Ammons poem as 'North Carolinian' may seem provincial and limiting, Archie Ammons is a poet better known in the large world of literature than in his home state, despite his induction into the North Carolina Literary Hall of Fame. Just recently, while in Columbus County, not far from where Archie grew up on a subsistence farm during the Depression, I met a retired college professor, an historian and native of Old Dock who had never heard of A.R. Ammons. He was incredulous that his home town was named in a poem, and delighted to see, for the first time, 'Alligator Holes down along about Old Dock.'

Archie—few who came to know him called him by any other name—said that this collection of his poems, when it was first published in 1994, was 'a literary makeover that feels like home.'

And North Carolina remained his home, despite the fact that he lived for the last 50+ years of his life in New Jersey and New York. He was always glad to visit, he enjoyed the idea of one day returning to live here, and he was proud that both his speaking and poetic voices stayed Southern. 'All my poems are North Carolinian,' he once told me, 'because I am.'

This new edition of *The North Carolina Poems* came about because of the persistent encouragement of Archie's widow, Phyllis. One of the last books published by the NC Wesleyan College Press, the first edition was out-of-print within a year of its publication. This edition benefits from the addition of several poems that had yet to be published in 1994 and two poems not previously collected. When *Tar River Poetry* published 'Making Fields' in 2009, it became the first Ammons poem to be published from the extensive Ammons literary archives housed at Cornell University, where for nearly 30 years he was poet-in-residence and an English professor. The poem was found there by Roger Gilbert, Archie's friend and Cornell colleague who is writing the official Ammons biography and who has been gracious in his sharing of Ammons finds.

The poems added to this new edition, like those in the first, include works which refer directly to places and people the poet knew in North

Carolina, but there are some which, poetically, simply feel like North Carolina (no doubt that Southern voice, that attention to place, a yearning for home), and still others which surely could have originated in any Carolina yard or woods or shore, though they came to Archie in New Jersey or New York.

I'm grateful to Jane and Larry Moore of Broadstone Books for their enthusiasm for this reprinting, and we are fortunate to once again have Jonathan Greene's elegant design. The poet's sometimes idiosyncratic punctuation and spelling have been retained: some poems end in colons, some in ellipses, others with no end punctuation at all. But that's all part of the fun of reading the work of this playful and philosophical Tar Heel called by William Harmon 'the state's greatest poet ever.'

But clearly, whether we in North Carolina understand it or not, his poetry has transcended regional identity. He's 'unquestionably among the best-loved poets of our time,' David Lehman says. Frederick Morgan adds that he's the 'best perceiver of the natural world we have,' a gift honed as a child exploring the fields, forests and ditches 'down in Carolina in a time & place that seem so long ago.'

When Archie was inducted into the North Carolina Literary Hall of Fame on October 15, 2000, he was not well enough to travel. I was selected to read four of his poems at the ceremony, attended by his sister, Vida, and two of her Columbus County friends. I asked Archie for suggestions; he named two and said I had to choose the other two. 'Alligator Holes down along about Old Dock' was an easy choice for the way it makes music of a wistful list of place names from his past, a list that's almost a secret code known only by those who grew up in rural Columbus County. It's suffused with quick, rich imagery from that life back home. Like most poems, it's much richer when read aloud, but this one especially needs to be read slowly, with emphasis on the wish that won't go away, that can't be fulfilled.

Before the induction, I asked Vida Ammons Cox and her friends if they would be kind enough to listen to me read the poems I would soon be presenting. Certainly, they said, and sat down in the sun-drenched Garden Room at Weymouth, that grand and beautiful estate created by James Boyd, where Faulkner, Wolfe, Fitzgerald, Sherwood Anderson, Robert

Ruark and Sam Ragan had been entertained. When I turned to 'Alligator Holes,' they held their collective tongues as I read. I could tell that I had butchered Nakina (say it with a long 'i' they would tell me soon) and Gause's Landing (Goss's, they would explain, not so much like *gauze* as I'd tried to say it, more like *toss*.) In their gracious correcting of my pronunciation, they were three ladies delighted to have the chance on this glorious day to say the names of places so close to their hearts and lives, and to say them over and over again, for themselves as well as for me, so that I would get them right: a litany in honor of their dear friend and brother.

—Alex Albright
Fountain, North Carolina
July 15, 2010

This book has been set in Adobe Garamond
designed by Robert Slimbach. Printing
& binding by Thomson-Shore, Inc.
Typesetting & design by
Jonathan Greene.

☙